MARCH   APRIL

Ff   Hh
Gg   Ii

JULY   AUGUST

Nn   Pp
Oo   Qq

NOVEMBE

Vv
Ww

Antler, Bear, Canoe

LITTLE, BROWN AND COMPANY
BOSTON TORONTO LONDON

Antler, Bear, Canoe

A NORTHWOODS ALPHABET YEAR

Betsy Bowen ❖

First Edition

Library of Congress Cataloging-in-Publication Data
Bowen, Betsy.
  Antler bear canoe: a northwoods alphabet year / Betsy Bowen. —
1st ed.
    p.   cm.
  Summary: Introduces the letters of the alphabet in woodcut
illustrations and brief text depicting the changing seasons in the
northern woods.
  ISBN 0-316-10376-4
  1. Nature — Pictorial works — Juvenile literature. 2. Seasons —
Pictorial works — Juvenile literature. 3. English language —
Alphabet — Juvenile literature. [1. Alphabet. 2. Nature.
3. Seasons. 4. Forests and forestry.] I. Title.
QH46.B69   1991
574.5′43′097 — dc20
[E]   90-33754

Joy Street Books are published by Little, Brown and Company (Inc.)

10 9 8 7 6 5 4 3 2

WOR

Published simultaneously in Canada by Little, Brown & Company (Canada) Limited

Printed in the United States of America

The pictures in this book are woodblock prints, made by carving the design and the big
letters, backwards, into a flat block of white pine, rolling black ink onto the block, and
then printing on a Vandercook No. 4 letterpress housed at the Historic Grand Marais
Art Colony. The colors are then painted on each print.

This is a book of the things I see around me where I live, in the northwoods of Minnesota. As you go through the alphabet, you will also go through the year, from winter to spring to summer to fall to winter again, just as we do here.

I hope you will enjoy seeing what life is like "back here in the woods with the mooses and the meeses," as an old Finnish logger, Wesley Warren, used to put it.

Betsy Bowen
GOOD HARBOR HILL

to Ginny,
who lived every minute fully

Antler

Once in January I found a moose antler in the forest. Now it is a feeder for the birds. Each winter moose lose their antlers, and each summer they grow them back.

Aa

Bear

The black bears here sleep from November to April. In January the cubs are born in the den while the mother bear is sound asleep.

Bb

Canoe

All winter long the canoe sits under the snow while the lakes are frozen. During the cold evenings, we dream of next summer's canoe trip.

Cc

Dogsled

Winter is a happy time for the sled dogs; they love to run and pull, hauling supplies or running races. Sometimes they go all night, with the light on the musher's head pointing out the trail.

Dd

Evening

Evenings are cold in February.
Inside we stay warm, reading or doing
schoolwork, waxing our skis, or ordering
summer garden seeds from a catalogue.

Ee

FEBRUARY

Fishing

In March the ice is thick and hard, strong enough to snowshoe or drive a snowmobile on. Fish living under the ice are eager to bite on a lure.

Ff

Grader

Each time snow falls, the road grader starts before dawn to plow the roads before the school bus comes. One winter the plow blade got too close to the edge of the road and knocked the mailboxes over.

Gg

MARCH

Hare

The snow is melting fast in April, and the snowshoe
hare is changing from white to brown,
in patches, like snow on brown earth.
Sap is running out of the maple trees.
Time to make maple syrup!

Hh

Island

In spring, when the thick lake ice is beginning to break up, it's safest to put one foot in the canoe and one foot out and scoot across from the island to the shore.

I i

Junk

In May, as the snow melts, all the junk shows up.
Sometimes we find treasures we had forgotten
about, but always there are things to load up
and take to the dump.

Jj

MAY

Kayak

The ice is gone now, and water is high in the lakes and rivers from melted snow. Time to go for a paddle and look for ducks along the shore, building their nests in the marshy places.

Kk

Loon

Loons will be returning to their nests in June to lay one or two eggs. Both parents will take turns sitting on the eggs until they hatch, around the Fourth of July.

L1

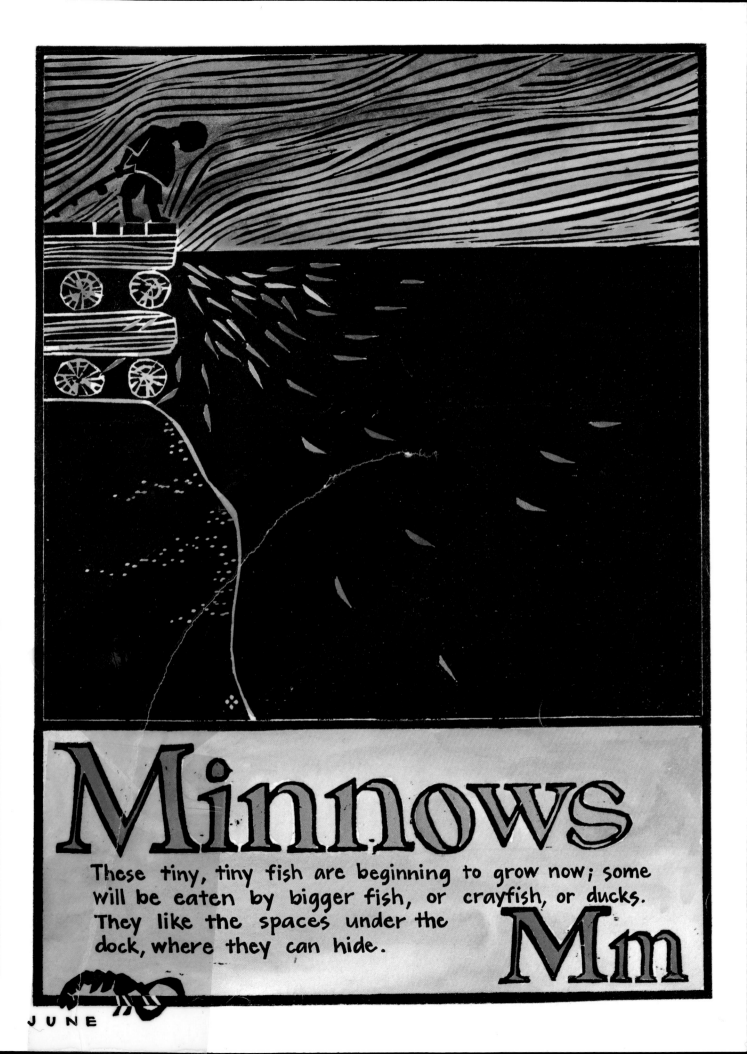

Minnows

These tiny, tiny fish are beginning to grow now; some will be eaten by bigger fish, or crayfish, or ducks. They like the spaces under the dock, where they can hide.

Mm

JUNE

Northern lights

The best northern lights we ever saw were in July one year, red and pink and neon green, dancing and tickling the stars. There must be sounds, too, I thought, only my ears can't hear them.

Nn

Outboard

We'll take the boat with the outboard motor to get to where the fish are. At a good spot we'll stop and fish for walleye or pike or trout.

Oo

Pond

One August beavers built a dam in the swamp
behind the house, and a pond formed there.
We keep the canoe at the edge of the pond,
but the paddles are tied high in a tree because
last year a bear chewed one up.

Pp

Quiet

If we ⟶ stand at the edge of the pond and listen, we can hear only a few quiet sounds . . . cattails moving in the wind, a duck splashing, a beaver's tail slapping the water.

Qq

Rendezvous

Many years ago, French Canadian fur trappers came to the fort nearby to trade and celebrate. This get-together was called a rendezvous. We go to the old fort each year to see the reenactment.

Rr

Saw

Cold weather comes back in September. We cut firewood to keep us warm all winter. When we stop our chain saw to add gas and oil, we can hear our neighbor's saw way off through the woods. A line of geese is flying back south. Summer is over. Time for school.

Ss

SEPTEMBER

Trees

The leaves are yellow and red and orange in October. Fall storms come and blow them off the trees. Berries ripen and become food for birds and bears to fatten up on before winter.

T t

Upstairs

Now that the first snow has fallen, we need our winter boots with thick felt liners, ski boots, ice skates. The down jackets are upstairs, too, and mittens, hats, scarves, long underwear— so many things to put on when we go outside.

Uu

Visitors

November is a brown and gloomy month here. It's time for visits to cheer us all up. Neighbors will come for potluck. Someone has been hunting, so we will have grouse for supper, and wild rice harvested from a lake, and beans from the summer's garden.

Vv

Wolf

With a few inches of snow on the frozen ground now, we'll see the tracks of the big timber wolves and the smaller brush wolves, called coyotes. The wolves themselves are harder to spot.

Ww

NOVEMBER

eXplore

There are many places where no one goes much, places with no paths and no roads, good places to explore in December. "Why, our backyard goes all the way to Hudson Bay," my dad used to say.

Xx

DECEMBER

Yarn

Cold weather now, time for sitting around the fire talking with friends and knitting yarn into mittens, socks, hats, sweaters, to keep us warm and to give as presents. Telling stories makes the knitting go faster.

Yy

DECEMBER

Zero

Temperatures are down to zero now. One last armload of wood to feed the fire for the night.

And so one year concludes in the northwoods, and another year begins.

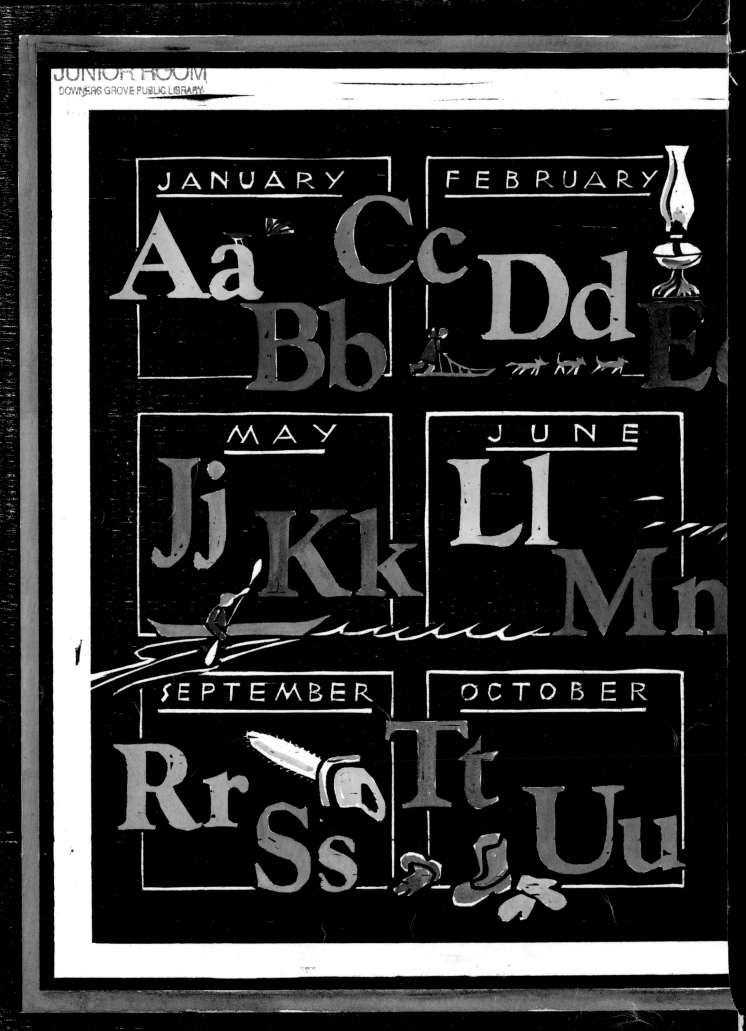